Unashamed Spirit, Untamed Heart
Blank Book

Art by
Tracy Brown

Use the blank side for doodles, diagrams, artwork, and more.
Use the lined pages for journal, notes, to do lists.
There is no wrong way to use your book!
You know that's right!!

Unashamed Spirit, Untamed Heart Blank Book/ Phyl
Campbell & Tracy Brown

ISBN:
978-0-359-83023-7

Printed in the United States of America

This book belongs to

_____

_____